THE *DIARY OF A WIMPY KID* SERIES

DIARY
of a
Wimpy Kid

THE GETAWAY

by Jeff Kinney

THORNDIKE PRESS
A part of Gale, a Cengage Company

GALE
CENGAGE Learning

Farmington Hills, Mich • San Francisco • New York • Waterville, Maine
Meriden, Conn • Mason, Ohio • Chicago

Recommended for Middle Readers.
Wimpy Kid text and illustrations copyright © 2017 Wimpy Kid, Inc.
DIARY OF A WIMPY KID®, WIMPY KID™, and the Greg Heffley design™ are trademarks of Wimpy Kid, Inc. All rights reserved.
Book design by Jeff Kinney
Cover design by Chad W. Beckerman and Jeff Kinney
Thorndike Press, a part of Gale, a Cengage Company.

Thorndike Press® Large Print The Literacy Bridge.
The text of this Large Print edition is unabridged.
Other aspects of the book may vary from the original edition.
Set in 16 pt. Plantin.

**LIBRARY OF CONGRESS CIP DATA ON FILE.
CATALOGUING IN PUBLICATION FOR THIS BOOK
IS AVAILABLE FROM THE LIBRARY OF CONGRESS**

ISBN-13: 978-1-4328-4372-4 (hardcover)
ISBN-10: 1-4328-4372-9 (hardcover)

Published in 2017 by arrangement with Amulet Books, an imprint of ABRAMS

Printed in the United States of America
1 2 3 4 5 6 7 21 20 19 18 17

TO ANNIE

DECEMBER

<u>Sunday</u>

The worst part of having someone tell you about their vacation is trying to pretend you're HAPPY for them. Because no one wants to hear about all the fun they DIDN'T have.

The only vacations I want to hear about are the ones where things went WRONG. That way, I don't feel bad for missing out.

Well, my family just got back from vacation, and believe me, if I could've stayed home, I WOULD'VE. But I didn't have a choice.

A few weeks ago, this vacation wasn't even supposed to HAPPEN. We were just having a normal December, and I was really looking forward to Christmas.

But Mom and Dad were getting all stressed out about everything we had to do to get ready for the holidays. We were WAY behind on decorating the house, and nothing was going the way it was supposed to.

I'm sure we could've gotten our act together in time for Christmas. But one night an ad came on TV that TOTALLY turned our holidays upside down.

The commercial was for this place called Isla de Corales, which is where Mom and Dad went for their honeymoon. And the reason I know that is because every time an ad for that place comes on TV, the two of them get all kissy-faced.

It makes me uncomfortable thinking about Mom and Dad before they had us kids. And I wouldn't HAVE to if Mom didn't break out their honeymoon album every year on their anniversary.

The night after that ad came on, Mom and Dad made an announcement. They said that THIS year, we were gonna SKIP Christmas and all go to Isla de Corales instead.

When I asked how we were gonna get our gifts to the resort, Mom said the trip WAS our gift.

10

I thought that sounded like a TERRIBLE idea, and I was surprised Dad was on board with it. He usually doesn't like to spend a lot of money, and I was sure this resort was gonna cost a FORTUNE. But he said he was sick of the cold weather, and he wanted to escape to someplace warm.

Personally, I don't have a problem with cold weather. In fact, generally speaking, the worse it is outside, the happier I am.

I figured Manny and Rodrick would help me talk some sense into Mom and Dad, and we'd put a stop to this idea. But those guys weren't any help at ALL.

So I had to accept that we weren't gonna have a normal Christmas at home. But what I REALLY didn't like was that we had to FLY to this place. I'd never been on a PLANE before, and I wasn't crazy about the idea of locking myself in a metal tube.

Nobody ELSE seemed worried, though, and two weeks later, on a night when we should've been hanging up our stockings and sitting around the fire watching Christmas specials, we were packing our suitcases for this island getaway.

Monday
We left the house around 8:00 on the morning of Christmas Eve. Dad was pretty uptight because he wanted to leave an hour EARLIER, but Mom said he was being ridiculous and we'd get to the airport in plenty of time.

It was only about twenty degrees outside, but Rodrick was already dressed for vacation.

It turned out Dad was right, we should've left earlier. Apparently, Christmas Eve is one of the busiest travel days of the year, so the roads were CHOKED with families driving to see their relatives. And nobody really seemed to be in the Christmas spirit, either.

What made things a lot worse was when it started to SNOW. After that, things slowed to a crawl. Mom and Dad started arguing over what time we should've left, and Dad almost missed the exit for the airport. He had to cut across three lanes of traffic, which didn't look easy.

When we reached the airport, the main parking lot was full. That meant we had to park in the economy lot, which was pretty far away. Dad said he'd drop the rest of us off at the curb with all the luggage and then come meet us after he parked.

When we got to the passenger drop-off area, it was COMPLETE chaos. We tried to unload our bags, but the cops weren't letting anyone stop for more than thirty seconds. And that just stressed everyone out and made things worse.

I had to get back in the van so I could help Dad with the rest of the bags. Ordinarily, that kind of thing would've been Rodrick's job, but since he was dressed for eighty-degree weather, he got out of it.

He was lucky he DID, too. When we got to the gate for the economy lot, Dad couldn't reach the ticket from his window. So he made me get out of the car to grab it.

Unfortunately, I didn't notice that there was a giant slush puddle on my side of the car until it was too late.

After we parked, we rolled our bags to the nearest shuttle stop, which wasn't a lot of fun.

16

The sign said the shuttle bus to the main terminal came every ten minutes. But there was no room for us in the bus shelter, so we had to wait outside in the freezing cold.

Twenty minutes went by without a bus, and Dad started getting really anxious about the time. He said we were just gonna have to WALK to the terminal, which was about a mile away.

17

I would've tried to convince Dad to wait a little longer, but my sock was starting to turn to ice, and I didn't wanna get frostbite.

Sure enough, once we got about a hundred feet from the shelter, the shuttle bus pulled into the parking lot. We tried to get the driver to stop, but he just blew right by us.

So we RAN to the shuttle stop, but we didn't make it back in time.

Now Dad was really worried about missing our flight. I told him maybe missing the flight wouldn't be the WORST thing to happen, but he didn't seem to be in the mood to hear what I had to say.

By the time we got to the terminal, we were both soaking wet and miserable. So when a pickup truck almost hit us in the crosswalk, it made Dad REALLY mad, and he let the driver know.

That just made the DRIVER mad, and he pulled his truck over and stepped out of his vehicle.

We didn't stick around long enough to talk things over with this guy. We ran in the opposite direction and blended in with some people standing on the sidewalk until the coast was clear.

Dad told me I could learn a lesson from this, which was to never lose your temper and do something stupid. But I took away a DIFFERENT lesson — when Heffleys get in trouble, Heffleys RUN.

The rest of the family was waiting inside the entrance to the terminal. Mom wanted to know what took us so long, and Dad wanted to know why she hadn't gotten in line with Manny and Rodrick and held a place for us.

It took twenty minutes for us to get through the check-in line. But when Dad put our big suitcase on the scale, the person at the counter said it was too heavy, and it was gonna cost extra money to check it.

But Dad said the airline was ripping us off and we weren't gonna give them an extra NICKEL. So we took some clothes out of the suitcase and stuffed them into our carry-on bags.

By the time we got everything sorted out, we had a half hour to get to our gate before our flight started boarding. And when we got to the security area, it was a total ZOO.

There were two lines — one for families and one for business travelers.

I guess Dad usually gets to go through the business lane when he travels for work, so he didn't seem to be too happy about being stuck with the rest of us in the family lane.

Anytime you add the word "family" to something, you know things are gonna be bad. And trust me, I've been to enough family restaurants to know what I'm talking about.

We waited in the security line a long time, and we finally made it to the front. But then some kid a few rows behind us started pressing the buttons on the poles that hold the barriers together.

All of a sudden, there was nothing keeping the lines separated, and for a second, no one moved.

But then things COMPLETELY fell apart.

By the time the security agents got all the zip barriers reconnected, we ended up at the BACK of the line. And the family with the kid who caused all the trouble was at the FRONT.

Now Mom and Dad were REALLY stressed, because our flight was supposed to leave at any minute. Dad begged one of the security agents to let us go to the front, but he didn't seem too sympathetic.

I thought we were going to miss our flight, so I didn't really see the point of going through security. But Dad said sometimes they leave the gate open until the last second, and we might still make it.

26

We finally got to the front of the line, and we put our bags on a conveyor belt. Then we took off our coats and shoes and put them into some plastic bins.

Manny saw what the rest of us were doing, and he started taking off HIS clothes, too. Luckily, Mom noticed in time and stopped him before he could go any further.

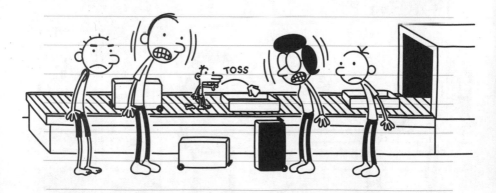

Manny wasn't finished causing problems, though. Apparently, he thought the conveyor belt was some kind of RIDE, and he was really upset when he found out that it WASN'T.

The people behind us were getting frustrated we weren't moving, but WE were being held up by the guy in front of us. He had to remove everything he had on that was metal, and it was taking him FOREVER.

Rodrick told me these machines can see through your CLOTHES, and then someone checks a screen to make sure you're not trying to sneak by with anything dangerous. All I can say is I wouldn't wanna be the person with THAT job.

It turns out the X-ray machine that sees through your clothes is only for grown-ups, and kids go through a metal detector instead. Still, I wasn't gonna take any chances.

Once we got through security, we grabbed our stuff from the conveyor belt and took off. Our gate was down on the lower level, so we had to take the escalator.

We couldn't even do THAT without causing a major problem. Manny's stuffed animal got stuck in the bottom of the escalator, and he had to press the Emergency Stop button so Mom could pull it free.

PRESS

Dad checked his watch and said we might still make it, so we ran for our gate.

But the gate was all the way at the other end of the terminal, and we knew we couldn't make it in time on foot.

Just then, a cart for handicapped passengers came along, and Dad stopped it and asked the driver if we could hitch a ride. The rest of us got on board before she could say no.

After that, it was smooth sailing. The terminal was pretty crowded, but people moved out of our way when they heard us coming.

The driver dropped us off at our gate, but the door was CLOSED. I thought that meant we had missed our flight and we could turn around and enjoy a nice Christmas Eve at home. But it turned out the flight was DELAYED, so all that stress was for nothing.

The reason the flight was delayed was because of the bad weather, and it was gonna be another HOUR before we got on the plane. We looked for a place to sit down in the boarding area, but people were hogging the seats.

Mom told me that once we got on the plane, we'd be in the air for about six hours, which was news to ME. I asked her for some money, and I bought a couple of magazines, some snacks, and headphones at a shop near our gate.

The only thing I needed that the store didn't have was SOCKS. My right sock was still soaking wet from stepping in that puddle, so I went into the bathroom to wring it out in the sink.

When I was done, my sock was still DAMP, and I really didn't wanna put it back on my foot. The bathroom had one of those high-powered hand dryers, and that gave me an idea.

I couldn't wait to get back home and start making some MONEY on this idea. I figured I could make a KILLING on rainy days.

The only problem with the hand dryer in the airport bathroom was that it was a little TOO powerful.

My sock started SMOKING, and then it went FLYING.

I decided I'd just get a new pair of socks at the resort, because there was no way I was gonna wear something I had to fish out of a URINAL.

When I came back from the restroom, they were making an announcement at our gate.

I figured they were ready to start boarding the plane, but they were just letting us know there was another DELAY.

And it went on like that for the rest of the day. Apparently, this storm was causing problems everywhere, and the plane we were supposed to fly out on was stuck at some OTHER airport.

I was starting to worry that my electronic device was gonna run out of juice while I was on the plane, so I looked for a place to charge it. But I guess everyone else was thinking the same thing.

The only available outlet was in an awkward place. But when your battery is at 15%, you gotta do what you gotta do.

Our plane finally arrived at the gate, and all the passengers who were on it got off. But if flying is supposed to be FUN, you'd never know it from the way these people looked.

The gate agent got on the loudspeaker and said we'd be boarding shortly. Then she said our flight was "overbooked," and they needed a few volunteers to give up their seats.

She said that whoever volunteered FIRST would get three hundred dollars and a free night at the airport hotel.

I didn't need to hear another word. I got to the desk before she'd even finished with her announcement and said I was her guy.

Unfortunately, Mom wouldn't LET me volunteer, and nobody ELSE stepped up, either.

So the gate agent increased the offer to
FIVE hundred dollars, and some woman
snapped it up right away. I just hope she
enjoys spending my money.

After that, the agent made ANOTHER
announcement. She said the flight crew
on our plane had worked too many hours
because of all the delays, and we had to
wait for a REPLACEMENT crew to come
in before we could take off.

Now everyone at our gate was MAD,
because what was supposed to be an early
flight was turning into an OVERNIGHT
one.

When the new flight crew finally arrived, they didn't look happy to be there. That's probably because they were expecting to spend Christmas Eve at HOME, so I knew EXACTLY how they felt.

After the crew got on board, they started letting passengers on the plane. My family got to go first, because they let people with young kids board before anyone else. But the gate agent stopped me at the door.

WILL YOUR BAG FIT?

She said my carry-on bag was too big to fit in the overhead bin, so it had to go down below with the rest of the luggage. That was fine with ME, because I didn't want to deal with my bag on the plane anyway.

When I got on board, I was pretty impressed. The seats were a LOT bigger than I expected, and they were covered in real leather.

I asked Mom what row we were in, but she said we needed to keep moving. She said this was the first-class section, and our seats were in ECONOMY.

But the economy section wasn't HALF as nice as first class. The seats were packed together, and they barely had any cushioning.

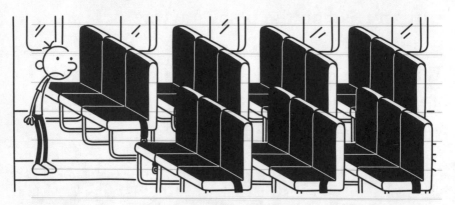

Mom said our seats were toward the middle of the plane, so we headed there. But Dad hung back in the first-class section. He said he got UPGRADED because of all his frequent-flier miles and that he'd catch up with us after we landed.

Mom didn't seem happy about this news. She said it wasn't fair for him to be in first class while we were in economy, so she said we'd all take TURNS sitting in Dad's seat during the flight.

But Dad said the rest of us weren't experienced travelers like him, and we wouldn't even know how to ACT in first class.

Luckily, there were other passengers trying to board, so Mom and Dad couldn't get into a full-blown argument right there in the aisle. Dad sat down in his seat, and we went to find ours.

The rest of us were all in the same row. Mom, Rodrick, and Manny sat on one side of the aisle, and I had the middle seat on the OTHER side.

Rodrick tried to get me to switch with him so he didn't have to sit by Manny, but I was happy right where I was. I didn't have a whole lot of leg room, but other than that, it wasn't so bad.

All the other passengers boarded after us, and people seemed pretty stressed trying to get their stuff into the overhead bins. So I was glad they took MY bag at the gate.

Everyone put away their bags and sat down in their seats. The pilot made an announcement that the doors were closing, and the seats to my left and right were still empty.

I couldn't believe my luck. As soon as we took off, I was gonna stretch out across all three seats and get myself a good night's sleep.

It was even BETTER than being in first class.

But right before the doors closed, one more couple got on board. And they had a BABY with them.

I didn't think these people would be in my row, because there were only TWO empty seats. But the baby sat in his mother's LAP.

See, if I were in charge of the airline, the rule would be one person per seat. Because if this couple had TWINS, it would've been completely out of hand.

I asked these parents if one of them wanted to switch seats with me so they could be next to each other. But the mother said she liked the window, and her husband said he liked to be on the aisle.

Right after that, the pilot came on the intercom. He said that before we took off, there'd be a brief safety video to show us what to do in case of an emergency.

I was already nervous about flying to begin with, and I didn't like hearing there might be an "emergency." So when the safety video played, I paid ATTENTION.

But as far as I could tell, I was the only person who DID. Everybody else completely tuned out.

The beginning of the video was just basic stuff, like how to fasten a seatbelt.

But after that, it got SERIOUS.

The video's narrator said that if there was a "loss in cabin pressure," oxygen masks would drop from the ceiling. Well, I don't know what "cabin pressure" is, but I didn't like hearing that we might LOSE it.

The people in the video didn't look bothered at ALL when the oxygen masks dropped down, though. In fact, they looked kind of HAPPY about it.

Then the video got even WORSE. The narrator said that in case of a "water landing," we'd need to evacuate the plane.

Now I was REALLY freaked out. I thought the whole point of an airplane was that it was supposed to stay in the AIR.

The safety video said there were emergency exits on the plane and the people sitting in the exit rows would need to open the doors so everybody could get out.

The emergency exit was one row behind me, and I realized the people sitting there weren't paying attention to the video at ALL. So I got them to put down their magazines and listen up.

The flight attendants didn't seem bothered that no one was watching the safety video. I figured they probably had their OWN exits, so if there was any trouble, I was gonna follow THEM.

The video showed the plane in the water with inflatable slides coming off the emergency exits. And they actually made it look FUN.

Then the video said our seat cushions doubled as "flotation devices," and each one had a whistle attached to it. Now I had questions, so I pressed the button above my seat to get the flight attendant to come over.

What I wanted to know was, if we landed in shark-infested waters, would it really be such a good idea to blow the whistle? It felt to ME like we'd basically be inviting the sharks over for a free lunch.

The flight attendant said I didn't need to worry, because all the seat cushions were coated with shark repellent, so they wouldn't even come near us.

I was pretty happy to hear that, but now I'm wondering if he was pulling my leg.

I don't really get the point of the whistles, though. It's not like anybody's gonna hear them if you're in the middle of the ocean.

And if you're lucky enough to have a cruise ship pass by, believe me, THOSE guys aren't stopping to pick you up.

After the safety video was over, I felt exhausted, and we hadn't even taken OFF yet. But a few seconds later, the plane started rolling down the tarmac, and the next thing I knew, we were in the AIR.

VROOM

I'm not gonna lie — I had my eyes shut during the whole takeoff. And I didn't even realize I was holding my breath until I almost passed out.

Once we leveled off, the couple sitting in my row started feeding their baby.

I was ALREADY nauseous from the takeoff, and the smell of mushy peas didn't help things.

I thought I might actually throw up, but I didn't know what to DO. Then I noticed this white paper bag in the seat pocket in front of me, and I figured out that's exactly what it's FOR.

The flight attendant already seemed annoyed with me, though, so I knew he wouldn't be too happy if I handed him a bag of vomit.

Somehow I managed to get through the feeding without throwing up. But I wish I could say the same thing for the BABY.

After the lady cleaned it up, she reached into her bag and gave the baby a couple of toys to play with.

One of the toys was a plastic hammer. And as soon as the baby got that thing in its hand, it started pounding on the WINDOW.

I've heard that if a window on a plane breaks, everything inside gets sucked OUTSIDE. And that didn't really seem like a good way to go.

So when the lady's head was turned, I swiped the hammer from the baby and tucked it under my seat.

Unfortunately, that set the baby off.

It turns out nobody likes a crying baby on a plane, and everyone started shooting us dirty looks. Luckily, the lady had a bottle in her bag, and that quieted the kid down for a while.

I was getting kind of hungry myself, so I pressed the button for the flight attendant and asked when we could expect to get FED. But he said meals were only for first-class passengers, and he gave me a bag of peanuts to hold me over.

That's when I remembered the snacks I'd bought before we got on the plane. But THEN I remembered that they were in my carry-on bag, which was stowed down below.

I guess Mom must've been thinking about food, too. Because as soon as the pilot said we had reached our "cruising altitude" and we were free to move about the cabin, Mom unbuckled her seatbelt and went up to first class with Manny, just in time for dinner.

I felt something cold and clammy touch my left elbow, and then something ELSE touched my RIGHT one. The guy behind me had taken off his shoes and socks and slid his feet through the spaces between the seats.

58

So I guess this guy decided it was OK to use my ARMRESTS as his FOOTRESTS.

I was starting to feel boxed in, and then the person in the seat in front of me tilted his seat all the way back, so it was just a few inches from my face.

I tried to tilt MY seat back, but I couldn't find the button to do it.

So I called the flight attendant and asked him where the button was. But he told me the seats in our row didn't tilt back because they'd block the emergency row.

Now I was starting to SWEAT. I thought I'd read a magazine to take my mind off feeling trapped, but the only thing in the seat pocket was a catalog for all this stuff no one needs.

Pizza Blanket

Night-time cravings? Satisfy them with the Pizza Blanket, edible bedding that's warm AND tasty!

Comes in pepperoni, extra cheese, and anchovies.

Snoozos

When you just can't sit through that boring meeting, Snoozos glasses make you look wide awake...even when you're anything but!

Phone Bubble

Protect your phone on rainy days with this clear plastic bubble!

The people on either side of me were
watching a movie, so I figured I'd turn
my screen on and check it out. The movie
looked like a comedy, but my headphones
were in my bag, and it was hard to
understand what was going on without
them.

I changed the channel to see what ELSE
there was to watch. One channel had a
show for little kids, and the baby next to me
got interested in what was on my screen.
And when I changed it to something else,
the kid started BAWLING.

When I changed the channel BACK, the baby stopped crying.

I guess I would've been OK with letting the kid watch the show, but the screen was WAY too close to my face. And the colors on the show were so bright that even when I put on the eye mask that was in the seat pocket, I could STILL see everything that was happening.

When the show finally ended, the baby started crying again. But there was no WAY I was gonna keep watching the show on repeat for the rest of the night.

So I decided it was the perfect time to take my shift up in first class.

But Rodrick noticed I was trying to make a move, and he got out of his seat before I had a chance to. And once he was up in first class, I knew I'd have to wait a while before I could swap places with him.

When Mom and Manny came back to their seats, I saw the door to the cockpit open behind them, and the pilot stepped out.

I thought there might be some kind of an EMERGENCY, so I pressed the button and asked the flight attendant what was going on. He said the pilot just needed to stretch his legs and use the bathroom, and the co-pilot had everything under control.

I didn't like the fact that we were down to one pilot, even if it was just for a few minutes.

Personally, I don't think two pilots is ENOUGH, even when they're BOTH in the cockpit. I guess the idea is that if one of them has a heart attack, then the other one is supposed to fly the plane.

But I asked the flight attendant what happens if the OTHER pilot freaks out and has a heart attack, too.

The flight attendant told me not to worry, because these planes are so high-tech they can practically fly THEMSELVES.

64

Well, I've heard pilots make a lot of money, so if what the flight attendant was saying is TRUE, then this could be the career for ME.

Once the pilot got out of the bathroom, I figured it would be a good idea for me to go, too. The only problem was, the man to my right was asleep, and I couldn't get over the guy without waking him up. So I went UNDER him, and believe me, that wasn't a lot of fun.

I walked toward the front of the plane, but before I even got to the first-class section, the flight attendant told me that economy passengers have to use the restroom in the BACK.

The bathroom in the economy section was really small, but being in there was a HUNDRED times better than being stuck in my seat. It was sort of like a tiny little apartment I had all to myself.

In science class, we learned that when human waste gets dropped out of an airplane toilet, it freezes solid. Some guy in my town once found a chunk of waste that fell from a plane, and he thought it was a METEORITE.

EXCLUSIVE: METEORITE CRASHES THROUGH MAN'S SHED

I think the guy was hoping to sell it for a lot of money, but once the thing thawed he found out what he had was totally worthless.

Once I was settled into the bathroom, I figured there was no reason to go back to my seat. So whenever someone ELSE came along to use it, I just made bathroom noises until they went away.

One person must've really needed to go, because they shook the door handle so hard that I thought it might actually break OFF. Then they went away. But a few minutes later, the whole BATHROOM shook.

Whoever this was needed to use the bathroom a lot more than I did, so I opened the door. But there was no one THERE. That's when I realized it wasn't just the bathroom shaking, it was the whole PLANE.

I thought we must've landed in the water or lost an engine or something. But then the pilot came over the intercom.

That didn't sound right to ME. I figured
what REALLY happened was that the pilot
fell asleep in his seat and kicked the steering
wheel or something, and then he came
up with this "bumpy air" excuse. Because
that's EXACTLY what I'd do if I were in
the same situation.

I guess the flight attendant could see that
I was pretty rattled. He said we were just
going through a little "turbulence," which
was perfectly normal for a flight like this.

Well, if this kind of thing is NORMAL, then there's no chance I'm ever becoming a pilot. Because if I were flying the plane, I'd be out of there at the first sign of trouble.

The flight attendant told me I needed to return to my seat and buckle up. But when I got back there, it was already occupied.

I didn't want to move the baby, because I knew it would just wake up and start crying again.

So I went up to the front of the plane to kick Rodrick out of first class and let HIM deal with the baby. But I couldn't GET to him. One of the wheels on the beverage cart had broken because of the turbulence, and it was blocking my way.

I was out of options, so I went back to my seat. Don't ask me how, but I was actually able to get an hour or two of sleep. And I was so tired, I didn't even wake up when we landed.

Tuesday

I was so worried about getting through the flight that I never thought about where we were actually GOING. But when I stepped off the plane, it was like walking into a whole new world.

I've gotta admit, as soon as I felt that tropical air hit my skin, I could understand why Dad was so eager to escape the cold back home.

We got our luggage off the conveyor belt in baggage claim, then followed the signs to where a big shuttle bus was waiting.

Even though the air outside felt GREAT, the air-conditioning on the bus felt even BETTER. And the seats in this thing were nicer than the ones in first class.

Once all the passengers boarded the bus, we headed to the resort. A video played on the overhead monitors, and it was about a MILLION times more fun than the one on the plane.

The video showed all the cool activities at the resort, and I wanted to do them ALL.

One of the activities was swimming with dolphins, and that's something I've ALWAYS wanted to do.

But there was a bunch of OTHER stuff that looked cool, too. I was hoping they might let us COMBINE activities so I could do everything before we had to go back home.

I felt kind of bad for being so negative about this trip up until then, and I turned around to tell Mom and Dad I was sorry. But I wish I had just kept watching the video instead.

When we stepped off the bus at the resort, the staff greeted us and handed Mom and Dad frozen drinks.

WELCOME TO PARADISE!

We gave our bags to these guys wearing white gloves, and they said they'd take them directly to our room. And I gotta say, I was IMPRESSED.

We went to the front desk, and the lady there explained how everything worked. She said the resort was "all-inclusive," so we didn't need to use cash or credit cards.

The way we paid for stuff was with these plastic cards that doubled as our room keys.

Mom and Dad told the receptionist they wanted to stay in the same building they'd stayed in for their honeymoon, but the lady said the resort had CHANGED since then. She said that now, the resort was split into two halves, the "Wild Side" and the "Mild Side."

The place Mom and Dad had stayed was on the Wild Side, and kids aren't allowed over there. So she showed us where our building was on the map.

78

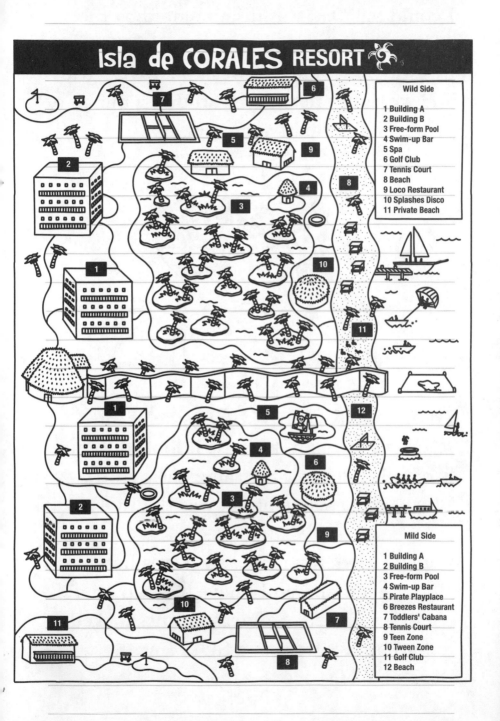

Isla de CORALES RESORT

Wild Side

1 Building A
2 Building B
3 Free-form Pool
4 Swim-up Bar
5 Spa
6 Golf Club
7 Tennis Court
8 Beach
9 Loco Restaurant
10 Splashes Disco
11 Private Beach

Mild Side

1 Building A
2 Building B
3 Free-form Pool
4 Swim-up Bar
5 Pirate Playplace
6 Breezes Restaurant
7 Toddlers' Cabana
8 Tennis Court
9 Teen Zone
10 Tween Zone
11 Golf Club
12 Beach

I could tell Dad was disappointed by the changes, but Mom said it was BETTER this way. She said this was a FAMILY trip, and we didn't need to be around a bunch of young couples partying, anyway.

I didn't really care WHICH side of the resort we were on, because it looked to me like both sides had the same basic stuff. What I really cared about was the ROOM.

Usually when my family stays at a hotel, we all share a room, and I have to sleep on a cot or a sofa bed. So I was pretty shocked to find out we were in a SUITE with PLENTY of space.

There were two rooms in the suite. We all
had to share one bathroom, but me and
Rodrick each had our own BED, which was
the main thing. All I can say is, Mom and
Dad must've dropped a LOT of money on
this trip.

There was a TV in the room I was sharing
with Rodrick, but even better than that,
there was a ROBE in the closet.

I called the robe right away, but Rodrick didn't even fight me for it.

Rodrick always makes fun of me when I wear Mom's robe back at home. But I think robes are COOL, and there are a lot of guys out there who would agree with me on that.

The shower in the bathroom was HUGE, and all the floors and sinks and everything were made of marble. There was a TV above the bathtub, and there was even a PHONE next to the toilet.

I figured if I could get room service delivered to the bathroom, I'd have everything I needed in one place.

From the balcony in Mom and Dad's room, I could see the pool over on the Wild Side of the resort, and it was really big.

It wasn't just some regular pool, either. It looked kind of like a river and had all these islands in the middle of it. Mom said it was one of the biggest "free-form" pools in the WORLD.

I was pretty excited about that, because I knew we had the same thing on OUR side of the resort. I wanted to go check it out, but first I needed to change my clothes.

I went to open the big suitcase, but it was LOCKED. I asked Dad for the key, but he said our suitcase didn't HAVE a lock. Dad looked at the tag on the suitcase, and it had someone ELSE'S name on it.

It turns out we had accidentally grabbed the wrong suitcase from baggage claim at the airport. Before it was too late, Dad called the airline to see if they still had OUR suitcase.

But the people at the airline said that since no one had claimed our bag, it was sent back to the address on the luggage tag.

It wasn't a TOTAL disaster, though. We'd moved some clothes from the big suitcase to our carry-on bags back at the airport, so we had a few things.

I had my bathing suit, but I didn't have a lot of OTHER stuff. My flip-flops and sunglasses were in the big bag, along with a bunch of other things I had packed. Dad said they sell the stuff we were missing at the resort store, so we went down to check it out.

But everything in the store cost five times as much as it would've back home, and Dad said he wasn't gonna pay those prices.

Mom said we could wear the same clothes every day and wash them ourselves. So the only thing we bought in there was a bottle of sunscreen and a toy pail and shovel for Manny to use at the beach.

Mom said it's really important to wear sunscreen at a place like this, because it's so close to the equator. But she didn't have to convince ME. I've seen what the sun can do to your skin, and I don't wanna look like a raisin when I'm older.

That's the reason I spend as much time indoors as I can. And later on in life, all my friends are gonna wish THEY had, too.

I thought the fact that we came during Christmas break meant we'd have the place to ourselves. But I guess a lot of people had the exact same idea.

It wasn't just the POOL that was crowded, though. There were people EVERYWHERE. I was really looking forward to relaxing in the hot tub until I saw it.

We found a few lounge chairs in the shade and put our stuff down. You could tell it was the middle of winter, because just about everyone looked out of shape, just like me.

Every once in a while, I think about exercising and getting really buff. But in the future, I'll bet everyone will just be able to take a pill and get fit without having to exercise, anyway.

Being in great shape will be NORMAL, and all the people who AREN'T fit will be the ones everyone's attracted to. So if I just stick with my current exercise plan, I'll be all set.

The pool was too crowded to go swimming, so I decided to just put a towel over my head and catch up on some sleep.

Even though it was hot out, there was a nice breeze, and I started to drift off. But right in the middle of my nap, some guy showed up and ruined the whole vibe.

This guy called himself the "Director of Fun," and apparently his job was to get everybody MOVING.

Unfortunately, this guy was good at his job, and somehow he roped ME into one of the activities.

But I wished he HADN'T, because there was a lot more touching than I was comfortable with.

SHAKE SHAKE

After the conga line ended, the Director of Fun said the next activity was the "Treasure Dive," and it was just for kids. I wasn't interested in doing some stupid kiddie thing, so I sat back down. But when he hauled out a giant bucket of COINS, that got my attention.

He told all us kids to line up at the edge of the pool, and then he started tossing giant handfuls of cash into the water. And it wasn't a bunch of PENNIES, either.

It was dimes and quarters, and I'm pretty sure I saw some SILVER DOLLARS in there, too.

By the time the bucket was empty, there must've been four hundred bucks sitting at the bottom of the pool. Everyone waited along the edge for the Director of Fun to blow his whistle.

When he did, it was a total free-for-all.

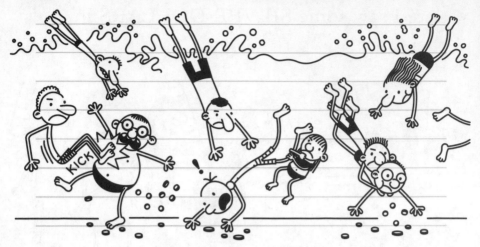

I managed to get about two dollars in coins on my first dive, and I put them at the edge of the pool near my lounge chair. But some sneaky kid swooped in and cleaned me out.

He wasn't the ONLY cheater, though. Some kid in the pool was actually wearing PANTS, and he stuffed his pockets FULL of coins.

That gave everyone ELSE the same idea, and now kids were stuffing coins wherever they COULD.

When it was all over, I think I ended up with about three bucks in change. After the kids cleared out of the pool, I figured it was a good time to get in the water and go for a relaxing swim.

95

I found a shady spot in the pool and leaned against the wall. But then I heard some rustling in the bushes behind me, and all of a sudden I was face-to-face with something that looked like it came straight from Jurassic Park.

I was out of there so fast, I actually SKIPPED across the water.

SPLOOSH   SPLASH   SPLISH

I told the lifeguard there was some kind of
DINOSAUR at the edge of the pool and he
needed to clear everyone out of there before
someone got HURT.

But the lifeguard didn't even seem fazed.
He said the giant lizard was just an
IGUANA, and they're all OVER the resort.
Then he said that sometimes the iguanas
even like to go for a dip in the pool.

Well, that changed EVERYTHING for me.
My feeling on giant lizards is that they
should be in a ZOO, not mingling with us
human beings.

I was DONE with the pool, so I asked Mom
if we could get some lunch.

She thought that was a good idea, and we found a place nearby that had an outdoor patio.

But the outdoor thing ended up being a problem. First of all, there weren't just iguanas at this place. There were geckos, salamanders, and who-knows-WHAT-else peeking out of the bushes.

It wasn't just LIZARDS, either. There were SLUGS, too, and we had to keep flicking them off the table with our utensils.

The waiter poured us glasses of water from a pitcher, but Mom told us all not to drink it. She said our stomachs aren't used to the microbes in the water down here, so we needed to get BOTTLED water instead.

98

But Dad said he'd be FINE because he's traveled all over the place and his stomach could handle ANYTHING.

I wasn't gonna risk it, though. I ordered a can of soda and poured it into a glass, and I got a burger and some fries, too.

When our food came, a few birds landed in the trees around our table. At first I was OK with it, because when the birds flew in, the lizards ran back into the bushes.

Then a bird that looked like it had an injured leg or something started hopping around on the ground near our table.

But it was all a big TRICK. The second we turned our heads to look at the bird on the ground, all the OTHER birds swooped in and went after our food.

We chased the birds off, but not before they got away with half our food. The only thing the birds DIDN'T touch was our drinks. It didn't matter, though. Some slugs were helping themselves to my soda, but luckily I noticed them before I took a sip.

I thought this place was supposed to be PARADISE, but so far it was a NIGHTMARE.

All I wanted to do was go back to the room and STAY there, but Mom said we were just getting started exploring the resort. Then Dad said he wanted to go back to the room, too. He said he wasn't feeling so hot and we could all probably use some rest after that flight.

We headed back to our building, but Dad had to make a pit stop at the restroom in the lobby. Then he had to go AGAIN in the bathroom next to the gym. So I guess Mom was right about the water.

The rest of the day wasn't much fun for ANY of us. When we finally made it back to our suite, Dad shut himself in the bathroom, and Mom sent me down to the store to get him some medicine for his stomach.

But the labels weren't in English, so I got him something that either CURES diarrhea or CAUSES it.

The medicine didn't seem to work, so we had to listen to Dad moaning and groaning all night.

I put on a movie in my room to try and drown out the sound. But my room was open to the outside, so the second I turned on the TV, a bunch of moths flew in and swarmed the screen.

We had to turn off the television AND all the lamps in the suite so the moths would fly back outside. Me and Rodrick ended up spending half the night just sitting there in the dark.

I was pretty tired anyway, so I figured I'd try to get a good night's sleep. But as soon as I got into bed, the music started up on the Wild Side of the resort. And those guys partied all NIGHT.

The crazy thing is, until that point I had forgotten that it was actually CHRISTMAS. I didn't know where this vacation was headed, but it seemed to me that there was nowhere to go but UP.

<u>Wednesday</u>

I probably could've slept for fourteen hours, but I was awake at the crack of dawn because of the racket a bunch of tropical birds were making right outside my window.

When I got out of bed, Mom was already awake. She said Dad spent all night in the bathroom and that we needed to leave so he could catch up on his sleep.

I was definitely ready for a fresh start, so I put on my bathing suit and headed for the door. But Mom said me and Rodrick needed to make our beds and straighten up the room.

I reminded Mom that we were on vacation, and the maid service would handle that for us. But she said that we weren't gonna live like ANIMALS just because we were on vacation.

I told Mom that the best part of being on vacation was having someone else clean up after you, but Mom said that this week we were gonna clean up after OURSELVES. Then she put the "Do Not Disturb" sign on the door so the maid wouldn't even come into the room.

I asked Mom how we were supposed to get clean towels and sheets, and she said we'd wash them in the bathroom sinks, the same way we were washing our clothes.

So Mom wasn't joking around about us doing our own laundry. In fact, Manny was in the sink scrubbing a pair of Dad's underwear, and I'm pretty sure he was using Rodrick's toothbrush to do it.

Personally, I think the best thing about staying in a hotel is getting clean towels and sheets every day. But Mom said hotels go through a ton of laundry detergent, and if we reused our towels and sheets, we'd be saving the environment.

That's when I noticed there were cards all over the bathroom that made you feel guilty about asking for clean stuff.

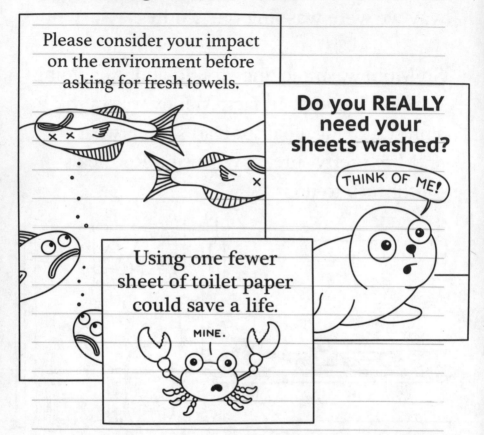

Please consider your impact on the environment before asking for fresh towels.

Do you REALLY need your sheets washed?

THINK OF ME!

Using one fewer sheet of toilet paper could save a life.

MINE.

Mom said we should all head down to the beach, but I wanted to hang back and take a shower. The truth is I wanted to take my TIME in there, and I knew if she was in the suite, she'd hassle me about using too much hot water.

What was crazy about the shower was that it was completely open to the outdoors. It took a minute to get USED to that, because I was worried someone might peek over the wall.

I guess there are people who are comfortable being naked right out in the open, but trust me, I'm not one of them.

I don't think it's right that you're BORN naked, because right away you're put in an embarrassing situation.

Once I got used to this open-air shower thing, though, I was ADDICTED. The shower had all these different settings, like "pulse" and "massage." I tried out every single one, but "rainfall" was probably my favorite.

I must've stayed in there for forty-five minutes. When I was done, I stepped out of the shower and put on my robe. But when I tried to put on my right slipper, there was something blocking my foot.

I held the slipper up and shook it, and a
giant SPIDER dropped out.

This was no ORDINARY spider, though.
That thing was as big as my HAND. When
it fell to the floor, I climbed up on the sink
so I wasn't on the same level as it.

I've had a thing about spiders ever since I was seven years old. One summer when I was in our garage, I found something in the corner that looked like a cotton ball, and I poked it with a broom handle.

Well, it wasn't a cotton ball. It was an EGG SAC, and it was filled with thousands of baby SPIDERS.

When I started school in the fall, the teacher had us fill out worksheets where one of the questions was what we wanted to be when we grew up.

Everybody wrote "astronaut" and "veterinarian" and and stuff like that. But not ME.

What's your favorite color?

BLUE

What's your favorite animal?

DOG

What do you want to be when you grow up?

EXTERMINATOR

Nowadays, whenever I see a spider, it takes me right back to when I was seven. I don't even like READING about spiders.

I'll tell you this — if I were one of the characters in "Charlotte's Web," it would've been a very short book.

I figured with MY luck, the giant spider on the bathroom floor was VENOMOUS. I've read that some spiders bite their prey, then wrap them up so they can eat them alive, which does NOT sound like a whole lot of fun.

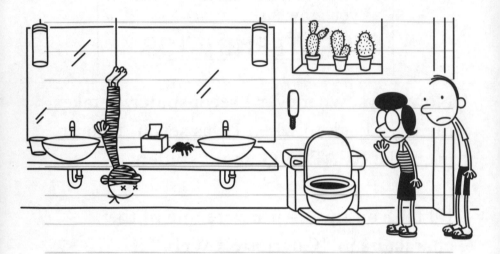

For some reason, the spider wasn't making a move. Either it thought it was camouflaged on the marble floor and I couldn't SEE it, or it was trying to figure out what to do next, just like I was.

I thought about throwing my slipper at it, but I was nervous I might miss and make it MAD. And even if I DID hit it, the slipper probably wouldn't have done any damage to this thing.

I called out for Dad to come help me, but all I got back was a weak groan from his bedroom. That's when I remembered the PHONE. I dialed 911, but I just got some prerecorded message.

The phone had all these other buttons, but none of the options were a great fit for the situation I was in. So I pressed the one for "Room Service," because I figured that was close enough.

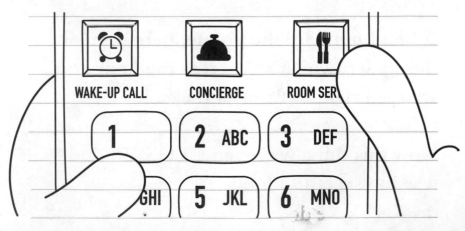

A lady answered, and I told her about the spider problem and how I needed her to send someone QUICK. But either I was talking too fast or there was some language confusion, because all she kept asking for was my BREAKFAST order.

Eventually, I gave up and just ordered scrambled eggs and a side of bacon. I honestly didn't care WHAT it took to get someone to come, as long as they came FAST.

When I hung up the phone, the noise jolted the spider, which ran across the floor and stopped right in front of the sink.

Now this thing was even CLOSER, and I was too scared to move.

I stood frozen for about fifteen minutes, barely breathing. But then the phone rang, and the sound surprised me so much I almost lost my balance.

It was the room service waiter. He said he had come to our suite to deliver my food, but there was a "Do Not Disturb" sign on the door, so he turned around and went back to the kitchen.

I told him to come BACK to the room and that he had permission to kick down the door if he wanted.

When I hung up the phone, the spider started running around again, and I was worried it was gonna figure out where I was and come get me. I looked around to see if there was anything I could use to DEFEND myself, but the only thing within arm's reach was a glass on the sink.

I realized that if the spider came close enough, I might be able to TRAP it. Sure enough, it ran right beneath me. And when it did, I managed to drop the glass on top of it.

CLINK

The spider wriggled around inside the glass, but it couldn't get OUT. I got down off the sink real slow and backed out of the bathroom, keeping one eye on the spider. But when I turned to leave, I smashed right into the WAITER.

All the noise got the spider moving again, and it took the glass WITH it. At first I wasn't worried, because it was still trapped inside. Then it crawled over the DRAIN where the floor dipped down a little, and that gave it just enough space to wiggle OUT.

That's when I found out the room service guy had the same problem with spiders that I did.

I knew it was up to me to deal with this thing, so I tried to trap it with the cover for the food. But the spider was zigzagging all OVER the place, and it wasn't easy.

Finally, I caught the spider by pinning it against the wall. I didn't really know what to do NEXT, because the second I lifted the food cover, that thing was gonna be off and running again.

Then I noticed that one of the spider's legs was sticking halfway out from under the lid.

I tried to move the lid to cover the whole spider, but I guess I pressed too hard, because the leg fell OFF.

The spider dropped onto the floor, and now it was going NUTS. I was running around on my tiptoes, trying to make sure I didn't get BIT.

Then the spider made a HUGE mistake.
It climbed onto the rim of the toilet, and
I knocked it in the bowl with my slipper
and slammed the lid shut. Then the room
service guy finished it off.

I gotta say, the two of us made a pretty
good team. And if I ever DO start that
exterminator business, I might have to look
this guy up.

After my encounter with the spider, I was pretty eager to get out of the room. I grabbed the map of the resort to find my way to the beach, but I got lost and ended up at the wall that separates the two sides.

I guess I understand why they'd wanna keep kids off the other side. But if you ask me, it kind of seemed like overkill.

I started to wonder if the room keys were actually tracking devices. That way, if any kids snuck over, they could put a stop to it.

KZAPP

When I got to the beach, it was PACKED with families. I decided the real reason the wall was built was to protect the couples on the OTHER side from seeing what was happening on OUR side.

Because if they knew what they were in for, there's no CHANCE they'd have kids of their own.

124

Mom had rented one of those covered
cabanas for our family to share. I wasn't
crazy about the idea of sharing a BED with
the rest of my family. But I talked myself
into it, because at least I'd be out of the
sun.

I remembered the beach cabanas from the video they played on the shuttle bus. They showed some couple having a romantic time watching the sun set.

Well, maybe that's how it was on the OTHER side of the resort, but on OURS, it was a whole different story.

CHEW CHEW

Mom told me and Rodrick she was taking Manny to the bathroom and that we needed to stay in the cabana. Mom said she got the last one and if we gave it up, somebody else would grab it.

One of the families that was waiting was WAY overdressed for the beach. I recognized the older kid from the Treasure Dive the day before. I guess nobody told these people you're not supposed to wear winter clothes in ninety-degree weather.

This family looked like they could really use some shade, and I felt kind of guilty. So I tried not to make eye contact.

Eventually, Mom and Manny came back, and Manny ran off to collect seashells.

Mom broke out the sunscreen and started putting it on me and Rodrick. I was glad Dad wasn't there, because he always gets mad when Mom does things for us that he thinks we should be able to do for OURSELVES.

I actually think this is all part of Mom's plan. I figure she doesn't want us to become too independent, because then we won't NEED her later on. I do think it could BACKFIRE on Mom, though.

Because if things keep going the way they're going now, there's a good chance me and Rodrick will go off to college not even knowing how to clip our own toenails.

This is one of the ways animals are different from people. In school I learned that once a bear cub is about a year and a half old, its mother sends it out into the wild to take care of itself.

But human beings live with their parents for eighteen YEARS before they're ready to go off into the world.

If I'm ever a parent, I'm gonna be like the BEARS. First of all, I'm not gonna spend a lot of time teaching my kids useless information, like the ABCs and colors and shapes.

The second my kid is old enough to cross the street safely and place an order at a fast-food restaurant, he's gonna be out of the house.

After Mom lathered Rodrick up, she told him he should go to the Teen Zone and try to connect with some kids his age.

130

I didn't think Rodrick would be interested, but he went to check it out. That got Mom all excited, and she said I should hang out with the tweens, who were on the beach doing a scavenger hunt.

But it was pretty obvious to me that the "scavenger hunt" was really just a beach cleanup in disguise, and I didn't want any PART in that.

When Rodrick left I was glad, because that meant more room in the cabana for ME. But a minute later Dad showed up looking really pale.

I thought he might still be dealing with stomach issues, but it wasn't that. He said when he went to use the toilet in our room, there was a giant SPIDER underneath the seat. So I guess we didn't get rid of it after all.

I asked Dad what happened NEXT, and he said he whacked the spider with a bathrobe that was on the floor. So there goes any chance I'm gonna wear THAT thing again.

I asked him if he KILLED the spider, and he said he wasn't sure. He said the spider VANISHED after he hit it.

Well, Dad's story pretty much guaranteed that I wouldn't be using our BATHROOM again, either. Luckily, there was an outdoor shower by the pool.

Dad seemed pretty shaken up by what happened with the spider, and Mom said he should lie down and take a few deep breaths. That's when Manny came back with his beach pail, and he showed Mom what he had collected.

I think Mom was expecting there to be a bunch of seashells in the bucket, but it was filled to the brim with hermit crabs, snails, and all sorts of OTHER living things.

And now these creatures were crawling all over our MATTRESS.

Mom scooped up the critters into the bucket and told Manny he couldn't keep these things as PETS, but he didn't seem to understand. Then she took the bucket down to the water to let them go.

SPLOOSH

Mom needed a way to distract Manny, so she took him down to the Activities Hut to see what kind of stuff they had for little kids. I wanted to do more than just lie around in a cabana all day, so I tagged along with Mom.

The one activity I really had my heart set on was swimming with dolphins. And the main reason I wanted to do THAT was so I'd have something to rub in Rowley's face when I got back home.

But the guy at the Activities Hut said that swimming with dolphins was really popular and it was totally booked. Mom asked if we could sign up for the NEXT day, but the guy told her it was sold out for the whole WEEK.

That wasn't the worst part, either. All the really FUN stuff, like jet skiing and parasailing, was only available on the Wild Side. And all the LAME activities were on the Mild Side.

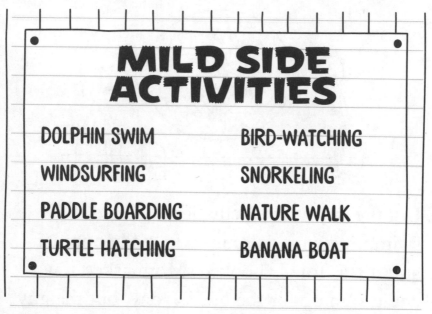

MILD SIDE ACTIVITIES

DOLPHIN SWIM	BIRD-WATCHING
WINDSURFING	SNORKELING
PADDLE BOARDING	NATURE WALK
TURTLE HATCHING	BANANA BOAT

But Mom didn't seem bothered. She signed us up for TWO activities, the banana boat and the turtle hatching.

Mom was ESPECIALLY excited about the banana boat. She said we could use the picture as our family Christmas card and send it out to everyone when we got back home.

136

It seemed like a pretty corny idea to ME, but I guess nothing could be as bad as the Christmas card Rowley's family sent this year.

Ho-Ho-Hope your family has a Merry Christmas!

Mom told me I needed to go get Rodrick, so I used the map to find my way to the Teen Zone.

But I probably could've found it WITHOUT a map.

Some of the teens were playing volleyball in the pool, and Rodrick was one of them. But the game was paused because one of the girls got her lip ring stuck in the net, and Rodrick was helping her get untangled.

I told Rodrick we needed to go, but he didn't seem to be in any hurry to leave. I finally got him to come with me, but I practically had to DRAG him away from his volleyball game.

We met everyone else down by the water, where they were getting fitted for life jackets. Mom gave her camera to the guy who was helping them and asked him to snap a picture when we passed by.

We got in the water and climbed aboard the banana boat, which was attached to a speedboat by a rope. We gave the driver the thumbs-up signal, and we took off.

Once we left the shallow water, we started to pick up speed. The water was kind of choppy, so it was hard holding on. Then we hit a big wave, and all three of us boys went flying off. The driver had to circle around so we could get back on.

When we got moving again, we went through the area where they had a water trampoline, and kids started using our banana boat as a TARGET.

Then one stupid kid landed smack in the middle of our boat and PUNCTURED it.

BLOOF

The banana boat was losing air fast, and the driver had to tow us back to shore. The guy that Mom gave her camera to took a picture, but I kind of doubt we're gonna use it for our Christmas card.

Season's Greetings

from The Heffleys

After we dried off, Mom said we should get some lunch. But the couple from the plane had already taken our cabana, and eating outdoors again didn't seem like such a good idea anyway.

I realized we hadn't eaten a real meal for two DAYS, and I didn't wanna eat anywhere that I HAD to worry about animals attacking my food.

Dad said we should go to the golf clubhouse, because it was the only indoor restaurant on the resort. Everyone seemed to like that idea, so that's where we went.

But when we got to the clubhouse, the manager said they couldn't serve us. He said the clubhouse had a dress code and that guys had to wear collared shirts and women had to wear dresses.

Dad told the manager we didn't HAVE those things, and the manager said that we could purchase them at the gift shop. But Dad said collared shirts cost fifty dollars each and there was no WAY he was gonna buy four of them just so we could have lunch.

So we had to find another place to eat. Rodrick wanted to just have some hot dogs in the Teen Zone, but Mom said she wanted to eat lunch as a FAMILY.

I was pretty sure they served burgers and fries at the swim-up bar at the pool, so we went there to check it out. But I had second thoughts about eating at the pool once we ordered. It was like having a meal in a bathtub with a bunch of people you don't know.

And it wasn't just PEOPLE, either. There was actually a MONKEY sitting at the other end of the bar.

Dad asked the bartender about the monkey, and she told us the whole sad story. She said this monkey used to live in a big tree on the resort with a bunch of OTHER monkeys, and he was kind of like their leader. But then this YOUNGER monkey came along and kicked him out.

The monkey didn't have any place to go, so one day he came to the bar, and people started buying him drinks. And he's been coming back every day since.

I really didn't know WHAT to think after hearing a story like that.

All I knew for sure was that I didn't feel
great about eating lunch while sitting in
monkey water.

There was some sort of big sports game on
the TV, and everyone at the bar seemed
really into it. But somehow Manny ended
up with the remote control, and he changed
the channel to a show for little kids.

Everyone wanted Manny to change the
channel BACK, but when Manny wants to
watch one of his shows, trust me, there's
nothing ANYONE can do about it.

The people at the bar were ready to RIOT,
so Mom scooped Manny up and we got out
of there before I even finished my burger.

Rodrick went back to the Teen Zone, and
Mom and Dad took Manny to the suite so
he could take a nap.

I really didn't want to go back to the room and risk running into that SPIDER again, so I decided to spend the rest of the afternoon in the arcade.

I had to make the coins I'd collected in the Treasure Dive last two and a half hours. But there were some kids in the arcade who could've lasted for DAYS in there without spending all of their money.

When it started to get dark, I figured I should head back to the room. But I ran into Mom, Dad, and Manny on the footpath halfway between the arcade and our building.

Mom said we were all gonna go down to a bonfire on the beach, and after that, we were gonna watch the turtle hatching. But first we needed to find RODRICK.

This time we ALL went into the Teen Zone to look for him. By now it was pretty dark, though, so it wasn't easy to spot him. But when we DID, I don't think he was too thrilled to see us.

On the way to the beach, Mom told Rodrick this was a FAMILY vacation, and it wasn't the time or place for "teenage romance."

Rodrick said this thing with the girl was
SERIOUS and they planned to spend as
much time as they could together.

I was kind of surprised, because I thought
Rodrick would be turned off by the whole
idea of romance after spending a few days
at the resort. Who knows? Maybe one
day he'll be back to this place with HIS
family.

We got down to the beach, where a bunch
of families had gathered around a bonfire.
But the experience wasn't fun because of
the BUGS. At first it was the gnats, which
flew in our eyes and mouths.

Then it was the sand fleas, which bit our ankles. And then it was the MOSQUITOES, which were the size of hummingbirds.

Whoever came up with the idea of calling this place "paradise" must've had a good sense of humor. Back home, human beings are at the top of the food chain. But at Isla de Corales, everything eats PEOPLE.

I was definitely ready to go back to the room, because at least THERE I only had to deal with ONE bug. But then the nature guide came through and said anyone who signed up to see the turtle hatching needed to follow her to the dunes.

The nature guide explained what we were about to see. She said that a mother turtle digs a hole in the sand dunes and then lays eggs in it, and a few months later, the eggs HATCH. Then the baby turtles head to the ocean.

She showed us a little pile of white eggs buried in the dunes and said there were LOTS of piles just like this one. She said the problem was that we don't know exactly WHEN the eggs will hatch.

It was DARK out, and I was afraid I was gonna accidentally step on an egg. So I took a few steps back to get out of the way, and when I did, something crunched under my foot.

Luckily, it was just a seashell. But still, my stomach was in KNOTS.

I'm not a fan of reptiles in general, but I decided I would make an exception for turtles.

Let's face it: The only reason we were out there to watch the baby turtles hatch was because they're CUTE.

Trust me, if this was a SNAKE hatching, it would be a totally different situation.

Just when I was getting ready to tell Mom we should give up and go back to our room, the eggs started hatching one by one.

Everybody got really excited, but the nature guide told us to stay quiet and get out of the way. She said the turtles find their way to the ocean by seeing the moonlight reflecting on the water.

But everyone ignored the nature guide and turned on their cell phones, and the camera lights made the turtles go every which way.

Mom was really enthusiastic, because she said we were witnessing the "miracle of life." She asked where Rodrick was, but no one knew. Dad said the last time he saw Rodrick, he was in the tall grass in the dunes.

And that's where we found him.

That SHOULD'VE been the end of the night, but it wasn't. When we got back to the room, we found out that Manny had pocketed one of the baby turtles while no one was looking, so Dad had to bring it all the way back to the beach to set it free.

Thursday

I guess Mom wasn't too happy with the way
our family vacation was going so far, because
after breakfast she said she was gonna take a
"spa day."

That sounded like a GREAT idea to me,
and I told Mom I was gonna tag along.
I've always wanted to get a massage, and I
figured this was my big chance.

But Mom said she needed time to
HERSELF and the rest of us were on our
own. That meant WE had to watch Manny.

Once Mom left, the three of us tried to figure out what to do. Manny was too much to handle, so I suggested we just drop him off at the Toddlers' Cabana and let the people who worked there deal with him.

Dad liked that idea, because he said he wanted to get in a workout at the gym. He told me and Rodrick we were responsible for getting Manny to the Toddlers' Cabana, and then he left.

The path took us right past the wall that separated our half from the Wild Side. I guess some kids were trying to get a peek at what was over there, but the landscapers put a stop to it.

FWOOSH

I asked Rodrick what he thought was on the other side, and he said he already KNEW. He said some of his friends in the Teen Zone told him that all SORTS of crazy stuff goes on over there and there's even a beach where people sunbathe without any clothes on.

He said there's a HOLE in the wall and if you look through it, you can see the other side. But I knew Rodrick was just trying to trick me, because he's told me this kind of thing BEFORE.

159

One summer when we were at the town pool, he told me that if I peeked over this cinderblock wall, I could see into the ladies' locker room.

Well, I BELIEVED him, and I've been trying to erase that image from my mind ever since.

We brought Manny to the Toddlers' Cabana, and the kids inside were making puppets. I told the person in charge we were dropping our little brother off for the day and we'd be back later.

The counselor said the only requirement for a drop-off was that the kid was potty-trained, and I told him that Manny WAS.

160

But Manny must really not have wanted to make puppets, because he got himself out of it.

Rodrick said I had to watch Manny by MYSELF, because he was gonna go check out the activities in the Teen Zone. But I knew he was just going there to meet up with that girl.

I was not happy that I got stuck with Manny. I didn't want to take him to the beach, because he'd just start collecting pets again.

So I took him to the Pirate Playplace, which was a splash zone for little kids.

It was actually PERFECT, because I could relax on a lounge chair and keep an eye on Manny while he played. I even ordered a grilled cheese sandwich and some french fries from a waiter who came by.

But I wasn't able to enjoy my meal. Some kids on the miniature pirate ship figured out that if they blocked one of the water cannons, they could make the other one shoot TWICE as far.

So I had to move to a lounge chair that was farther away. But when I sat down, I realized I had lost track of MANNY. I eventually spotted him in the middle of the wading pool, all by himself.

I knew I had to go in there and get him, but I really didn't WANT to. With the number of little kids in the pool, I knew EXACTLY what was in that water.

When I was little, I used to pee in the baby pool all the TIME. In fact, there's a framed photo of me in the family room using the pool as a potty.

Mom says it's her favorite picture of me, because I look so HAPPY. But I've never told her WHY.

One summer, they put some chemical in the pool that turned green if anyone peed. So that put an end to THAT.

I needed to figure out a way to get to Manny without touching the water, so I found a raft and a pool noodle and paddled out to him.

But I only made it halfway across when a bunch of little kids decided it would be fun to climb onto my raft. I tried fighting them off with the noodle, but there were just too MANY of them.

Then they teamed up to flip me OVER.

I got Manny out of the pool and then spent twenty minutes scrubbing every inch of my body in the outdoor shower.

SCRUB SCRUB

But five seconds after I finished drying off, I was WET again. The kids in the pirate ship figured out that if they plugged TWO cannons, they could get some SERIOUS range.

While I was drying off a SECOND time, we
bumped into Mom. And after her morning
at the spa, she seemed like a whole new
person.

She said that while she was getting her
massage, she came up with a GREAT idea
for how we could spend time as a family.
She booked a private cruise for all of us,
and she said the boat was gonna be at the
dock in half an hour.

That wasn't a lot of time, so we had to split up to track down Dad and Rodrick. I told Mom that Dad was at the gym, so she went there to get him.

I found Rodrick exactly where I expected to, and believe me, he owes me for not letting Mom get to him FIRST.

We met Mom and Dad down at the dock. Dad wasn't too happy with Mom, because apparently this boat cost a lot of money to rent. But Mom said it was WORTH it, because this cruise was gonna be the highlight of our trip.

When I hear the word "cruise," I think of a yacht or at least a souped-up sailboat.

But the boat that Mom rented didn't look like anything special.

The boat came with its own captain, so I guess that was SOMETHING. When we got on board, he handed us all life jackets, and after we put them on, we pulled away from the dock.

The first thing I noticed was that the boat had a glass bottom, which I was not comfortable with at ALL.

s boat didn't look like it was in such
eat shape to begin with, so I was worried
ne glass was gonna crack and we were all
gonna sink to the bottom of the ocean.

In fact, if I had to guess, I'll bet 50% of all
shipwrecks are glass-bottom boats just like
the one we were on.

Once we got out on the ocean, the captain asked Mom where she wanted to go. The captain said there were some private islands we could explore, and Mom said we should go to one of THOSE.

But it turned out the "private" islands weren't really private, so we didn't bother sticking around.

The captain said there was a reef nearby that wasn't usually crowded and we could do some snorkeling.

That meant we'd have to go into the actual ocean with all the OTHER stuff swimming around in there, so I wasn't in love with the idea. But nobody else seemed concerned.

Once we got out to the reef, the captain dropped anchor, and he handed us each a snorkel, a mask, and some flippers.

I asked if he had any HARPOONS or other weapons that we could use to defend ourselves from sharks.

He said sharks don't go near the reefs, but I said I'd bet if they saw a defenseless family splashing around, they'd be happy to make an exception.

He told us the reason that sharks don't come near the reefs is that the coral is SHARP and that WE shouldn't touch it, either.

That was the FIRST red flag. But it got a whole lot WORSE.

He said there was a pretty good chance we'd see some stingrays underwater. He said it was OK to touch their fins but we should keep our thumbs away from their mouths, because they can mistake them for food and bite them clean off.

Then he said the stingrays' tails are poisonous, so we should probably watch out for THOSE, too.

The captain wasn't FINISHED, though. He said there were a bunch of OTHER things we needed to look out for. Then he showed us what everything looked like on a big chart.

There was some scary stuff on that thing, but it wasn't the BIGGEST creatures that freaked me out, it was the SMALLEST one. And that was the BOX JELLYFISH.

I saw this show called "World's Most Venomous Creatures," and they had the box jellyfish at the top of the list. If you get stung by one, your heart can stop, and then you're pretty much finished.

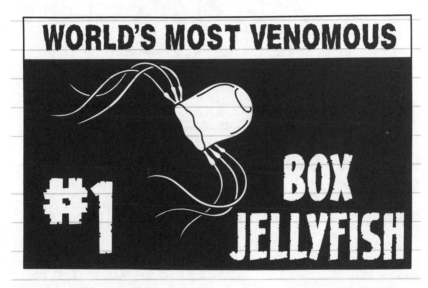

I told Mom I didn't think it was worth risking death just to see a goldfish in the wild. I think she could tell I was worried, but she wouldn't let me off the hook that easy.

She said I just needed to get in the water long enough to take one family picture and then I could get back in the boat.

Mom still wanted that photo for the Christmas card, and I could tell she wasn't gonna take "no" for an answer.

I told Mom I'd stay in just long enough for ONE picture, and if someone BLINKED, that was just tough luck. She agreed, and then we got in the water one by one. I was the last person in.

SPLOOSH

The captain couldn't figure out how to work Mom's camera, and he was taking FOREVER.

I really didn't like the feeling of not knowing what was swimming underneath me, so I took a peek underwater. I'm glad I did, because it was actually kind of AMAZING. I could see why people liked snorkeling and scuba diving so much.

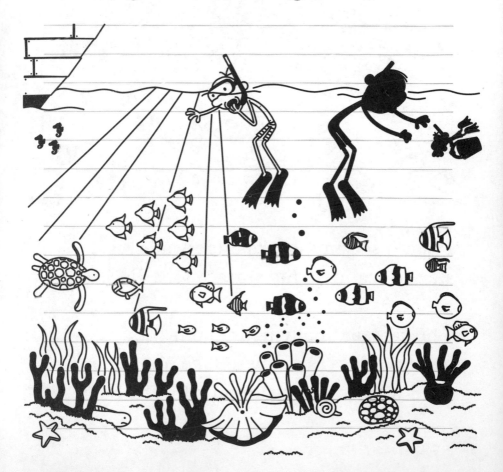

A big school of blue and green fish surrounded me, and the fish were darting all over the place, changing directions two times a second.

At first I thought it was COOL, but then I realized that this is how animals behave when they're trying to avoid a PREDATOR.

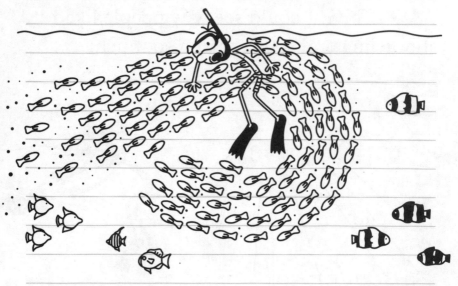

I didn't see any sharks underwater, so I started scanning the surface for FINS.

The captain finally figured out Mom's camera and was ready to take our picture, but I was already swimming for the boat.

Just then, a sea horse swam right in front
of my mask, and it surprised me. My
snorkel dipped beneath the surface, and I
accidentally took a HUGE gulp of water.
And I'm 95% sure that I swallowed the sea
horse along WITH it.

Now I was in a full-blown panic. I think I
might've actually DROWNED if the
captain hadn't pulled me up into the boat.

Once I was on board, I coughed up a lot of water but no sea horses.

Mom climbed aboard to find out what was wrong. She could see I wasn't looking so good, and she told the captain we should go back to the resort so I could get checked out by a doctor. After everybody else climbed in, we headed back.

The ride was really choppy, and if I hadn't ALREADY been sick, that would've done it.

We made good time, and the captain dropped us off at the dock.

He had already called ahead to the resort's doctor, who was waiting for us. When I told him what had happened, I thought for SURE he was gonna send me to the nearest hospital to get my stomach X-rayed.

But he checked me out and said I seemed OK. Then he told me it wasn't very likely I swallowed a sea horse and I'd be perfectly fine.

I really didn't like how casual this guy was being about the whole thing. In fact, he seemed a lot more concerned with Mom and Dad than he did with ME.

The doctor took a look at them and said it looked like they were seasick. Then he gave them each a pill and said they'd feel better after they got a little rest.

All I can say is, if anything happens to me later on, I hope this doctor knows he had a chance to DO something about it, but DIDN'T.

Mom and Dad found a few empty lounge chairs by the pool, and we sat down to rest.

But then the Director of Fun came through with a conga line, and he tried to get us to join.

He couldn't take a hint, though, and kept circling our area. But he stopped cold when he noticed something in Manny's pail.

It looked to ME like a clear plastic bag floating in the water. But the Director of Fun lifted the pail to take a closer look.

It turned out it wasn't a plastic bag at ALL. It was a JELLYFISH. And not just ANY jellyfish, either. It was a BOX jellyfish.

The Director of Fun ran to the nearest lifeguard, who started blowing her whistle. Then all the other lifeguards started blowing THEIRS. And you have never seen so many people get out of a pool so FAST.

My family decided it might be a good idea for us to get out of there, too.

On our way back to the room, we noticed that Rodrick wasn't with us. Mom thought he probably snuck off to hang out with that girl, but when we went to the Teen Zone, he wasn't there.

That's when we realized nobody had seen Rodrick in a WHILE. In fact, I didn't remember him being on the boat ride back from the reef. And neither did Mom or Dad.

That meant he was still OUT there.

So we ran back to the dock as fast as we could. Our boat was already out on another trip, but Mom talked to the guy who operated the banana boat and told him what happened. We climbed on board the speedboat, and he took us to the reef.

Sure enough, we found Rodrick exactly where we left him. He was ALIVE, but he was as red as a LOBSTER.

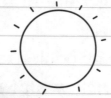

When we got back to the resort, the doctor said Rodrick had sun poisoning and needed to drink lots of water and get some rest. Then he gave Mom a bottle of aloe to help Rodrick with his burn.

But the aloe didn't really seem to help Rodrick. Mom sent Dad to the store to find something that would, and we spent the rest of the night taking turns rubbing popsicles on Rodrick's back.

Friday

The next morning, Dad went out to get another box of popsicles, and he came back with some news. He said they had drained the whole pool to find the jellyfish, and they were just starting to refill it. But it would be three DAYS before it was ready to use.

I thought it would be smart for us to hide out in the suite for the rest of the trip, because people would be looking for the family who ruined everybody else's vacation. But Mom said we weren't gonna spend the rest of our time indoors.

She told Dad he should take Manny to the
Pirate Playplace, and she told me to see what
activities were planned in the Tween Zone.

I didn't really want to go back out there,
but I guess it was better than risking
another run-in with the spider.

I went down to the Tween Zone, hoping
the activity might be a video game
competition or something like that. But the
counselor was rounding everyone up to play
TENNIS.

At first I thought about turning around,
because I wasn't in the mood to get all
sweaty.

Then I remembered that Rowley plays tennis at his country club, and I thought it might be fun for me to learn so the two of us could hit some balls around over the summer.

The counselor who was organizing the game was named Rodrigo, and he took us over to the tennis courts.

I thought Rodrigo was going to stay and teach us how to play. But the second we were all through the gate at the tennis court, he LOCKED it.

That's when I realized these "activities" were just a way to get kids out of their parents' hair for a few hours.

The tennis court was a giant CAGE, and we were basically in prison for the next hour and a half. And we couldn't even play tennis anyway, because Rodrigo didn't leave us with any RACKETS.

He did leave us with BALLS, though. There must have been three hundred of them in a basket in the middle of the court. At first, kids started playing catch, but it didn't take long for it to turn into a giant free-for-all.

I took cover by the fence with some other kids who didn't wanna get hit in the face with a tennis ball. But all that did was make us TARGETS.

So we started fighting BACK. Somebody figured out how to turn on the ball machine, and we used it to defend ourselves.

I'm never on the winning side of this kind of thing, and I gotta say, it was actually a lot of FUN.

But then everything came to a screeching halt. One of the kids who was in the conga line the day before recognized me and told everyone it was MY family's fault they had to drain the pool.

I explained to everyone that it was all a big accident and that my little brother just wanted a jellyfish as a pet. But I guess these guys were mad about the pool situation, and they were happy to have someone to blame.

I had to get OUT of there, but the gate was locked. So the only way to go over it was to CLIMB.

In phys ed at school, I can't even get up the rock wall they have in the gym. But now that my life was on the line, I scaled that fence like I was SPIDER-MAN.

After I cleared the fence, I ran to the counselors' building to get help. But Rodrigo was totally USELESS.

I didn't feel safe outdoors anymore, so I ran back to our building.

Everybody in my family was in the suite when I got there.

We were kind of in a bad spot. I didn't wanna leave the room, and Rodrick couldn't be out in the sun anyway.

Mom said maybe we should call off the trip and head back home a day early. But Dad said we paid a lot of money for this trip and he refused to leave the resort until we had at least ONE decent meal.

None of us wanted to eat at an outdoor restaurant because of the stupid birds. And we couldn't eat at the golf clubhouse, because we didn't have the clothes for it.

Just then, there was a loud crash on the other side of the room.

The big suitcase that belonged to somebody else was split open on the floor. And there were clothes EVERYWHERE.

Whoever this suitcase belonged to must've been a family just like us, because there were clothes in all different sizes.

But they weren't just beach clothes. There were also the kind of clothes you'd wear to church or a nice restaurant.

I looked at Dad, and I could tell he was thinking what I was thinking: These clothes were our ticket to getting into the golf clubhouse.

Mom said she didn't feel right about wearing someone else's clothes. But Dad said that after we were done using them, we'd pack everything back up and make sure the suitcase got to the family it belonged to.

I think that made Mom feel better, so we started trying things on. The only person who couldn't find clothes that fit was RODRICK. But Mom said he needed to stay covered up from the sun anyway, so she gave him a robe and a shirt to put on over it.

I gotta say, when we stepped out of our building, we looked pretty SHARP. Rodrick's outfit even worked in its own way.

We walked toward the clubhouse, and I kept my eye out for any tweens who might recognize me. But we made it to the restaurant without any run-ins.

THIS time, they let us in. And I had the best meal I've eaten in my whole life.

After we finished dessert, none of us really wanted to head back to the room. So we had a little fun on the putting green first.

The truth is, my family NEVER has a good time together. So for a second there I could kind of see how this family vacation thing is supposed to work.

But what I've learned is that nothing good ever LASTS. A security guard drove up to the putting green in a golf cart, got out, and said we needed to come with him.

When Dad asked him WHY, the security guard said that another family at the restaurant had reported us for wearing their CLOTHES.

For a second, we didn't know what to do. Then I remembered what I learned back at the airport — when Heffleys get in trouble, Heffleys RUN.

I got in the driver's seat of the security guy's golf cart, my family piled in, and we took off, leaving the security guard in our dust.

But it turns out that a golf cart makes a lousy getaway car, especially if you're climbing a HILL.

The security guard caught up with us less than a minute later, and I don't think he even broke a sweat.

202

He made us go back to our room and hand the suitcase over to the family it belonged to. We also had to return the clothes we were wearing, and I gotta say, it wasn't our proudest moment.

Personally, I think the embarrassment
should've been punishment ENOUGH.
But the security guard said that theft isn't
tolerated at the resort and we had to pack
our bags and leave the grounds immediately.

Dad tried to explain what REALLY
happened, but this guy wasn't in a
listening mood. And once we had all our
stuff packed, he drove us to the airport
HIMSELF.

When we got to the airport, Dad went to
our airline's customer service desk and told
them we needed to fly home a day early.

But the customer service lady said that all the flights for the day were sold out, and we were just gonna have to wait until the NEXT evening to fly home.

That was a problem, because we didn't have anywhere to STAY for the night.

Dad called the airport hotel, and they said there was only one room available. So we spent the last night of our vacation in a tiny room. And I had to share a bed with Rodrick, who was sticky from popsicle juice.

<u>Saturday</u>
When we woke up in the morning, I figured
we were in for a long day. Our flight wasn't
until 8:00 p.m., and there was nothing to
do at the airport. But at breakfast, Mom
and Dad surprised us.

They said we were gonna go BACK to the
resort for the day.

Mom and Dad had talked it over the night
before, and neither one of them liked the
way things had ended. They decided they
wanted to have a "do over" and leave on a
high note.

Mom said the most important thing was
that we get that family picture. She said she
knew the PERFECT spot on the beach,
and as soon as we got to the resort we were
gonna head straight there.

I thought the whole thing was a crazy idea, because I didn't see how we were even gonna get past the front desk. But Dad said he had a plan, and he'd tell us what it was when we got there.

We took the free shuttle back to the resort, and we watched that video again. I realized the reason everything looked so FUN was because they never showed any actual FAMILIES.

When we got off the bus, Dad told us his master plan to sneak onto the property. And I gotta say, it wasn't really that impressive.

But it actually WORKED. Once we got past the lobby, we went to the pool area. There wasn't anyone swimming, because they were still filling it.

We quickly found out where everyone ELSE was — down at the beach. But it was so crowded, no one looked like they were having any FUN.

Mom wanted to get the family picture, but she didn't want other people in the shot. So we went to the sand dunes, where nobody else would be in the background.

But that's where we ran into Rodrick's girlfriend.

I felt kind of BAD for Rodrick, ESPECIALLY after Mom asked the girl to take our picture with her camera.

I'm not sure we're gonna be able to use the photo as our Christmas card anyway, since Mom usually likes everyone to be SMILING in those.

After the family picture was out of the way, we went back down to the beach. Rodrick was sulking, but the rest of us had FUN.

We worked up an appetite, and we were ready to eat. The problem was, the security guard had taken our room keys when he kicked us out of the resort. So we couldn't actually PAY for anything.

A family in one of the cabanas had some leftover pizza and fries. So we used what we learned from the birds and helped ourselves to some food.

After that, Dad said we needed to start heading back. Mom wanted to get a few more pictures at the sand dunes before we left, so we went there.

But I think we pushed our luck, because we ran into some OTHER people we knew.

The second that family saw us, they ran off, and I knew they were gonna report us to security. So we left the scene as fast as we could.

I don't know where the REST of my family went, but I headed toward the BEACH. I figured there were so many people there, I could just blend in. But when I saw a security guard running toward me, I PANICKED.

I ran into the water and swam to the area
where the windsurfers were. I had no idea
how to USE one of those things, but I
thought it was my only shot at escaping.

I got on the board, then pulled the sail up
out of the water. And as soon as the sail was
upright, I started MOVING.

I found out the way to steer the thing
was by pulling on the big handle that ran
across the sail. I figured as long as I was
headed AWAY from the beach, I was
doing OK.

Then a big gust of wind caught the sail, and I didn't have enough strength to steer it the way I wanted it to go. I was moving FAST and picking up speed.

Up ahead, there were some buoys that marked a roped-off area of the water. I pulled back on the handle with all my might, but I couldn't avoid the ropes.

I guess there must've been a fin on the bottom of the windsurfer, because something got caught on a rope. And when it did, the whole thing tilted over and splashed into the water.

I tried to stand the sail back up, but it was hard to do it in the choppy water. Then something brushed by my LEG, and I FROZE.

Two seconds later a FIN appeared, and then another, and another. I was completely surrounded, and I thought I was about to become lunch for a school of sharks.

That's when I realized I was in the DOLPHIN enclosure. I was so happy that I forgot all about how I got there.

But when a security boat pulled up alongside me, it brought me back to reality.

I gave up on windsurfing and swam for shore. But the beach was a lot less CROWDED than I remembered it being a few minutes before.

I found out WHY when I got there. I'd accidentally crossed over to the WILD SIDE. And those guys didn't look too happy to see a kid with a camera on their private beach.

Now security guards were coming at me from every direction, and I hightailed it out of there. It wasn't just the security guards who were after me, though. It was the SUNBATHERS, too.

I sprinted across the sand into the pool area, which looked a lot like the one on OUR side, only the pool had WATER in it.

I had a pack of people right behind me. So I jumped over a stone wall and took cover in a cluster of bushes.

When I pushed through to the other side, I thought I was in the clear. But then I came smack up against the WALL.

There was a HOLE in this part of the wall, and you'd never believe who was on the other side of it.

PSST!

I got my family's attention and told them I needed help.

Then I put my fingers in the hole to try to pull the board loose. Dad pushed from the other side, and the wall actually opened a crack. But it wasn't big enough for me to squeeze through.

I could hear the security guards on their walkie-talkies right on the other side of the bushes, and I knew it was just a matter of SECONDS before they found me.

So I tried climbing UP the wall, but I couldn't get a foothold. Then I saw Rodrick's HEAD pop over the top. He reached out his hand, and I jumped to grab it. He started to haul me up, and I thought I might actually make it.

But then a seven-legged SPIDER crawled out of Rodrick's bathrobe and down my arm, and I lost my grip.

220

When I hit the ground, I thought I was
done for. But then the section of the wall
I was trying to get over came crashing
DOWN. I was lucky I didn't get crushed
by the stampede pouring in from the Mild
Side.

We took advantage of all the confusion and made our way to the exit. There was a security station at the side of the resort, and the only reason we were able to slip past the guards was because of all the craziness going on over at the Wild Side pool.

Once we were off the property, we flagged down a cab and asked the driver to take us to the airport.

We hit some turbulence on the flight back, but after everything ELSE we'd been through, a little rough air didn't even faze me.

<u>Sunday</u>
It's been a few days since we made it back home, and Mom's already working on the photo album. And from the pictures, you'd think we had a great time.

But any chance of us ever going BACK to the resort is completely gone. I went on the website to show Rowley where I spent my Christmas vacation, and there was a big picture of my family on the home page.

I couldn't read the words that went with it, but I'm pretty sure I got the general idea.

ACKNOWLEDGMENTS

Thanks to everyone at Abrams, especially Charlie Kochman, who cares as much about book twelve as book one. Big thanks to Michael Jacobs, Andrew Smith, Chad W. Beckerman, Susan Van Metre, Liz Fithian, Carmen Alvarez, Melanie Chang, Amy Vreeland, Samantha Hoback, Alison Gervais, Elisa Garcia, and Josh Berlowitz.

Thanks to Jason Wells and Veronica Wasserman for your friendship. Thanks to Kim Ku for breaking new ground in Wimpy Kid design.

Thanks to the whole Wimpy Kid team: Shaelyn Germain, Anna Cesary, and Vanessa Jedrej. Thanks to Deb Sundin and the staff at An Unlikely Story.

Thanks to Rich Carr and Andrea Lucey for your support and friendship. Thanks to Paul Sennott for all your help.

co Jess Brallier for your mentorship getting me started as an author.

anks to everyone in Hollywood, including lvie Rabineau, Keith Fleer, Nina Jacobson, Brad Simpson, Elizabeth Gabler, David Bowers, and Greg Mooradian.

ABOUT THE AUTHOR

Jeff Kinney is a #1 *New York Times* bestselling author and a six-time Nickelodeon Kids' Choice Award winner for Favorite Book. Jeff has been named one of *Time* magazine's 100 Most Influential People in the World. He is also the creator of Poptropica, which was named one of *Time* magazine's 50 Best Websites. He spent his childhood in the Washington, D.C., area and moved to New England in 1995. Jeff lives with his wife and two sons in Massachusetts, where they own a bookstore, An Unlikely Story.